TO THE TEACHER

There are increasing demands on young children to write. The exercises in this book are designed to help them develop better sentence skills and organize their ideas, especially when writing about factual material.

While the format of this text is that of a workbook, many of the exercises on sentence structure should be done orally first, whether in a classroom, a small group, or a tutorial. The grammar terminology introduced is usually the conventional terminology: there is little point in a child's mastering one term, only to have to learn a different one later on in school. Sentence skills can be developed most effectively when practiced in isolation, rather than as part of a composition lesson.

The paragraph assignments are designed to encourage children to write about things with which they are likely to be familiar. The step-by-step approach will enable all of them to become more confident writers. Length, which students of all ages worry about, is chiefly a matter of organization. When students are composing, they do best if allowed to let their ideas flow without worrying too much about the mechanics, which can be addressed separately. Composition work is an exercise in thinking, not in spelling.

Students who fail to use capitals and punctuation consistently can be helped by being asked to put a box around every capital and a circle around every period before they hand in their work. After a few weeks of doing this, they can put a check mark in the margin to show that they have checked for correct capitalization and punctuation. Writing on every other line is always helpful as it makes proofreading easier. Spelling errors are often difficult for students to find. At a more advanced stage, a teacher can put a dot in the margin for every spelling error. The task of the students in the end is to see how many errors they can correct on their own.

While the exercises in this book alternate between those involving sentence structure and grammar and those involving composition skills, they may be done in any order. For instance, you might want to start the paragraph exercises early in the year. Merely completing an exercise may not result in mastery, but by following the patterns established in the text, teachers can devise additional exercises of their own.

As in the other books in this series, the emphasis is on expository, rather than creative, writing. Exposition is important for all advanced academic work, is a teachable skill, and impacts the comprehension of texts.

Diana Hanbury King

Writing Skills

Book A

EDUCATORS PUBLISHING SERVICE
Cambridge and Toronto

For Shirley Kokesh and the joy we share in teaching.

Designer: Karen Lomigora
Editor: Theresa Trinder
Managing Editor: Sheila Neylon

Printed in the U.S.A.
ISBN 0-8388-2049-2
978-0-8388-2049-0
10 11 12 13 PPG 15 14 13

CONTENTS

THE SENTENCE

You use sentences all the time, whenever you speak, read, or write. This book will help you understand how sentences work.

A sentence is a group of words that states a complete thought. Every sentence begins with a capital letter and ends with a punctuation mark, usually a period.

Read the sentences below. Each one expresses a complete thought, begins with a capital letter, and ends with a period.

1. I am learning to play the drums.

2. Carver Elementary School has a great gymnasium.

3. Marty likes to eat chicken and rice.

> → **Exercise 1**

Read the following groups of words and decide whether each one is a complete sentence. If the group of words is a complete sentence, put a ✓ in the box. If the group of words is not a sentence, put an ✗ in the box.

Examples: ☑ my brother is in the seventh grade

☒ the hot dog stand

☐ 1. I understand it now

☐ 2. coming around the mountain

☐ 3. unless they can read the sign

☐ 4. if you can help them

☐ 5. in the middle of the night

Here is some extra practice. Read each group of words and decide whether it is a complete sentence. Put a ✓ or an ✗ in the box.

☐   1. we adopted a new kitten

☐   2. very early in the morning

☐   3. they ran all the way home

☐   4. an enormous black spider

☐   5. Dan is my best friend

☐   6. when the train arrived

☐   7. the kids playing checkers

☐   8. the geese flew high in the sky

☐   9. ate a tuna fish sandwich

☐   10. she loves to fly kites

☐   11. they left school at three o'clock

☐   12. it rained all day

☐   13. people who like to sing

☐   14. Sam lost the ball

☐   15. hoping for a sunny day

→ **Exercise 3**

Now go back and look at the complete sentences you found in Exercise 2. In the spaces below, rewrite five of them so that they begin with a capital letter and end with a period. After you have written each sentence, draw a square around each capital and a circle around each punctuation mark.

Example: [M]y brother is in the seventh grade⊙

1. _____

_____

2. _____

_____

3. _____

_____

4. _____

_____

5. _____

_____

SUBJECTS

A sentence has two main parts: the subject and the predicate.

The subject is who or what a sentence is about. The subject often starts the sentence.

Read the sentences below. You will see that each subject is circled.

(My best friend) likes spaghetti.

(Our library) has a new children's room.

(These overalls) are too big.

→ Exercise 1

Read the following sentences. Then find the subject in each sentence and circle it.

1. My dog comes when I whistle.

2. My uncle went to the store.

3. Tim always comes to class late.

4. The duck dived under the water.

5. That cup is chipped.

6. The moon is full tonight.

7. She put her toys away.

8. Polar bears like cold weather.

9. Daffodils bloom in the spring.

10. Peter led the way to the ballpark.

11. The cow jumped over the moon.

12. That sweater needs to be washed.

13. The whole family enjoyed the movie.

14. The leaves need to be raked.

15. Summer is my favorite season.

NOUNS

The subject of a sentence always contains a word called a noun. Nouns name a person, place, thing, or idea. Plants and animals count as things.

Here are some examples of different types of nouns.

Person	Place	Thing	Idea
Dad	train station	book	happiness
friend	New York	dog	freedom
teacher	village	tree	love
Ms. Jones	beach	computer	friendship
dentist	movie theater	hat	belief

Each of these nouns is either a person, place, thing, or idea. Read each one and decide which category it belongs in. Write it in the correct place below.

airplane	town	moon	pride
joy	grass	Ms. Gray	Mr. Lee
dragon	tooth	Ohio	friendship
neighborhood	hope	cactus	health
Sally	peace	museum	teacher
grandmother	apartment	horse	doctor

Person	Place	Thing	Idea

Add two of your own nouns to each column.

Look at the following nouns. First, decide whether each is a person, place, thing, or idea and write your answer on the line. Then, on the second lines, write a sentence using each noun.

cloud _____

_____

_____

cow _____

_____

_____

Grandpa _____

_____

_____

freedom _____

_____

_____

city _____

_____

_____

SORTING NOUNS

A good way to understand nouns is to practice sorting them into groups, or categories.

→ Exercise 1

These nouns are animals. Read the list and sort each noun into the right group.

pigs	lions	hippos
tigers	cows	chickens
elephants	sheep	ducks
horses	giraffes	monkeys

Farm animals	Zoo animals

These nouns name different types of objects. Read the list and sort each noun into the group that tells where you would expect to find it.

pencils	desk	eraser	ice
cups	stove	plate	trays
pans	pens	salt	mugs
paper	crayons	spices	pencil sharpener

In the classroom	In the kitchen

10

These nouns name different places. If the noun is a specific place, like New York City, France, or Antarctica, it needs a capital letter. Read the list and sort each noun into the right group.

pond	state	los angeles	desert
town	woods	africa	australia
chicago	mississippi	england	egypt
city	paris	neighborhood	plain

Need capitals	Do not need capitals

 **Your Turn**

Use five words from the last exercise to write five sentences.

1. _____

   _____

2. _____

   _____

3. _____

   _____

4. _____

   _____

5. _____

   _____

PRONOUNS

Sometimes the subject is a word that takes the place of a noun, such as **it**, **he**, **we**, **she**, **they**, **I**, or **you**. These words are called pronouns.

Nouns: <u>Kate and Tom</u> went to the amusement park.

Pronouns: **They** went to the amusement park.

Noun: <u>The comic strip</u> was very funny.

Pronoun: **It** was very funny.

Noun: <u>Sally Ride</u> was the first American woman in space.

Pronoun: **She** was the first American woman in space.

→ **Exercise 1**

Rewrite the following sentences using a pronoun in place of the underlined nouns. Don't forget to begin with a capital letter and end with a punctuation mark.

Examples: <u>Mr. and Mrs. Jones</u> live across the street.

They live across the street.

<u>My friend and I</u> are working on a science project.

We are working on a science project.

1. <u>The new movie</u> is very popular.

_____

_____

2. <u>Harold</u> waited at the bus stop.

_____

_____

3. <u>Ms. Blackwell</u> is my favorite teacher.

_____

_____

4. <u>The roller coasters</u> are very scary rides.

_____

_____

5. <u>My family</u> took a trip to the San Diego Zoo.

_____

_____

6. <u>Jane and Mark</u> shared their sandwich.

_____

_____

7. <u>Dr. Lucas</u> said to get plenty of rest.

_____

_____

8. <u>Jon, Calvin, and I</u> helped clean up.

_____

_____

9. <u>The math problems</u> are difficult.

_____

_____

10. <u>The storm</u> will pass over the city.

_____

_____

Now write five sentences using one of the pronouns **I**, **you**, **we**, **he**, **she**, **it**, or **they** as your subject. Try to use a different pronoun for each sentence.

1. _____

_____

2. _____

_____

3. _____

_____

4. _____

_____

5. _____

_____

ARTICLES: *A, AN,* AND *THE*

The words **a**, **an**, and **the** often appear just before a noun.

They are called **articles**.

You can test if a word is a noun by seeing if it makes sense with **a**, **an**, or **the** before it.

A is used before words beginning with a consonant. Here are some examples.

> **a** parakeet
>
> **a** skyscraper
>
> **a** baseball game
>
> **a** city

An is used before words beginning with a vowel. Here are some examples.

> **an** instrument
>
> **an** astronaut
>
> **an** olive
>
> **an** umbrella

The is used before words beginning with any letter. It is different from **a** and **an** because it talks about one special thing.

If I say, "I went to <u>the</u> party," I do not mean just any party, but a special one.

Read the following nouns. Decide whether you should use **a** or **an** before each one and write it on the line.

Example: __*an*__ igloo

1. _____ pony

2. _____ elephant

3. _____ ice cream cone

4. _____ marching band

5. _____ parachute

6. _____ orange

7. _____ umbrella

8. _____ ant

9. _____ beetle

10. _____ oak tree

Look at these sentences and compare them. The first group of sentences uses **a** and **an.** The second uses **the.** How are they different?

I caught **a** fish

We visited **a** city.

An egg was cracked.

A package arrived today.

She sold **a** bicycle.

I caught **the** fish.

We visited **the** city.

The egg was cracked.

The package arrived today.

She sold **the** bicycle.

_____

_____

Now make up two groups of your own sentences. In the first sentence, use the article **a** or **an** before your noun. In the second sentence, use the article **the**. Compare your sentences. Do you see how the meaning changes?

1. Sentence 1

_____

_____

Sentence 2

_____

_____

2. Sentence 1

_____

_____

Sentence 2

_____

_____

SINGULAR AND PLURAL

Usually, nouns can be counted. If there is just one, we call it **singular**. If there are more than one, we call it **plural**.

→ **Exercise 1**

Label these nouns **s** for singular or **p** for plural. The first two have been done for you.

_p_ coats   _s_ car   ____ pencil   ____ teacher   ____ dishes

____ flower   ____ parents ____ buses   ____ children   ____ finger

____ song   ____ beaches ____ squares   ____ house   ____ wives

____ computer   ____ maps   ____ mice   ____ lawns   ____ truck

→ **Exercise 2**

Did you notice that most words make the plural by just adding an **s**? Some add **es** and some do something else. Find the six that do something other than add **s**. Circle them. Then write them on the lines below.

1. _____   4. _____

2. _____   5. _____

3. _____   6. _____

→ **Exercise 3**

Write the plural of these words by adding an **s** to the singular.

1. eraser _____

2. spider _____

3. cloud _____

4. street _____

→ **Exercise 4**

Now read the following plural nouns. Try to think of the singular noun for each one. Write it on the line. Be careful! A few of them are tricky.

1. nights _____   6. glasses _____

2. skies _____   7. babies _____

3. inches _____   8. halves _____

4. trains _____   9. bridges _____

5. women _____   10. teeth _____

Try using plural nouns in your writing. Create five sentences. Use a plural noun in each one.

1. _____

   _____

2. _____

   _____

3. _____

   _____

4. _____

   _____

5. _____

   _____

PREDICATES

You already know that the subject of the sentence tells who or what the sentence is about.

The other part of the sentence is called the predicate. **The predicate** tells more about the subject.

Sometimes it tells what the subject **did**, **does**, or **will do**.

The dog barked at the mail carrier.

Taylor walked his bicycle across the road.

My grandparents will arrive this afternoon.

Sometimes it tells something **that happens** to the subject.

She got an art set for her birthday.

The flag is flown from the Capitol.

The hamster was put in its cage.

Sometimes it tells what the subject **is like**.

Roses are red.

Our mail carrier is friendly.

The water was too cold for swimming.

Read these sentences. Underline the predicates. Then copy the predicates on the line below. On the next line, rewrite the sentence using your own predicate. Look at the example for help.

Example: My brother <u>helps me with my homework.</u>

My brother *helps me with my homework.* _____ .

My brother is playing kickball. _____ .

1. That dog chases cars.

   That dog _____ .

   _____ .

2. My friends look forward to recess.

   My friends _____ .

   _____ .

3. The pony trotted around the field.

   The pony _____ .

   _____ .

4. That chair is comfortable.

That chair _____.

_____.

5. People often lose their keys.

People _____.

_____.

6. My grandparents live in Mexico.

My grandparents _____.

_____.

7. The robin built a nest in the bush.

The robin _____.

_____.

8. Lemonade is made of lemons, sugar, and water.

Lemonade _____.

_____.

Read these sentences. Circle the subject and underline the predicate in each one. Look at the example for help.

Example: (Ann) practices karate every Saturday.

1. The rain fell all day.

2. The river is wide and deep.

3. Children have fun at the playground.

4. The woods are dark and cool.

5. That parrot talks a lot.

6. The rabbit ate all my lettuce.

7. My bed is comfortable.

8. The bus came late today.

9. I saw the squirrel in the tree.

10. The carpet is soft.

11. Seven is my lucky number.

Add a predicate to these words to write ten complete sentences. Remember to put the subject at the beginning of your sentence and the predicate at the end.

1. the puppy _____

_____

2. summer _____

_____

3. stars _____

_____

4. my sneakers _____

_____

5. that hat _____

_____

6. the kitchen table _____

_____

7. ducks _____

_____

8. my mom _____

_____

9. I _____

_____

10. my friends _____

_____

Did you remember to use capitals and punctuation? Re-read your sentences to make sure. Draw a square around each capital and a circle around each end punctuation mark.

Sometimes a word or group of words comes before the subject. Find the subject in each of these sentences and circle it. It may help to ask yourself, "Who or what is the sentence about?"

Example: All of a sudden, (the sun) came out.

1. Suddenly, the fish jumped out of the water.

2. In the morning, the cookies were gone.

3. At night, the birds go to sleep.

4. Soon, our lunch will be ready.

5. Fortunately, nobody was hurt.

6. Carefully, he lit a match.

7. Racing down the hill, Sally tripped and fell.

8. At last, the package came in the mail.

9. Tomorrow, the circus is coming to town.

10. After many weeks of travel, they reached the sea.

Complete these sentences by adding a subject and a predicate.

Example: High in the sky, *the kite flew.* _____ .

1. Late last night, _____ .

2. Luckily, _____ .

3. Without making a sound, _____ .

4. At the far end of the field, _____ .

5. Around the corner, _____ .

6. Pretending to be asleep, _____ .

7. Unfortunately, _____ .

8. Early the next morning, _____ .

9. In the middle of the road, _____ .

10. Everywhere in the world, _____ .

VERBS

The predicate of a sentence always contains a word called a verb.

Verbs are words that show action or connect two ideas in a sentence.

Here are some examples of different types of verbs. These are examples of **action verbs.** They will tell what the subject does, did, or will do.

ate   Mario **ate** three servings of broccoli.

travels   The Smith family **travels** to Oregon every summer.

dance   We **dance** together in the school play.

walked   Mr. Long **walked** all the way to the grocery store.

slept   I **slept** in a tent in the backyard.

There are other kinds of verbs called **linking verbs** and **helping verbs**. You will see these kinds of verbs often. These do not show action, but can be a very important part of a sentence.

Here are some common **linking verbs**. They link together the circled part of the sentence.

is	(Patty) **is** (my best friend.)
am	(I) **am** (nervous about the test.)
are	(We) **are** (third graders.)
was	(Ms. Kim) **was** (an architect.)
were	(You) **were** (very funny in the show.)

Here are some common **helping verbs**. They help give meaning to the verbs that follow.

has	Harry **has** (sent) me an e-mail.
have	I **have** (thought) about the problem for a long time.
had	We **had** (looked) everywhere for the keys.
can	Sandra **will** (ask) the clerk for help.
will	You **can** (have) some of my popcorn.

Read each sentence. Circle each action verb. Then write a sentence of your own using the action verb you circled.

1. They ran down the dirt road.

_____

2. My neighbor mowed the lawn.

_____

3. The man juggled five oranges.

_____

4. The deer leaped over the fence.

_____

5. Drink this glass of water.

_____

Now you know about nouns and verbs. Can you tell whether each of these words is a noun or a verb? Write each word in the right column.

throw	apartment	New Jersey	went	dinosaur
see	ball	gave	yelled	sailing
frog	Matt	kicked	draws	rushed
phone	erase	clothes	Maria	goldfish

Nouns	Verbs

34

Now write five sentences using one word from each column. You may make the nouns singular or plural.

1. _____

   _____

2. _____

   _____

3. _____

   _____

4. _____

   _____

5. _____

   _____

TENSE

Tense is a word that means time. Verbs change, depending on when the action happens.

Some verbs tell what is happening now, or in **the present**. Some verbs tell what has already happened, or in **the past**. Some verbs tell what will happen tomorrow, or in **the future**. Look at the following examples. Notice how the verb changes in each one.

present (happening now)	past (already happened)	future (hasn't happened yet)
I **am** happy.	I **was happy**.	I **will be happy**.
It **is raining**.	It **was raining**.	It **will rain**.
We **learn**.	We **learned**.	We **will learn**.

	acted	

Read these sentences. First, circle each verb. Then decide whether it is happening in the present, past, or future, and write it in the right column on page 36.

Example: Calvin (acted) in the school play.

1. They drove for two hours.

2. Dad will cook dinner tonight.

3. The birds in my garden are singing.

4. We are reading a wonderful story.

5. The water in the lake will freeze this winter.

6. Nobody knew the answer.

7. Many people will be on vacation.

8. The lights went out in our town.

9. She is practicing for the play.

10. Leaves blow in the wind.

Complete these sentences any way you wish. Be sure to use the right tense so that your sentence makes sense.

1. Tomorrow _____

_____

2. Soon _____

_____

3. Now _____

_____

4. Last week _____

_____

5. Yesterday _____

_____

6. Once upon a time _____

_____

7. Next summer _____

_____

8. Today _____

_____

9. A hundred years ago _____

_____

10. Late last night _____

_____

SUBJECTS AND PREDICATES

Let's review what you have learned about the subject and predicate.

The subject tells who or what the sentence is about.

The predicate tells what the subject does or what the subject is like.

→ **Exercise 1**

Here are some subjects and predicates. Make complete sentences by connecting a subject in the first column to a predicate in the second column. Your sentences may be silly!

Nobody	took a shower
Spider-Man	ate ten hot dogs
The old goat	was always late
My big sister	went to the movies
Everybody	lost their keys
A little toad	answered the phone
We	landed on the moon
The teacher	lives in my basement
The aliens	learned to yodel
My cat	slept all day
A bunch of grapes	played the flute
The sea lion	told a funny joke

Copy your five favorite sentences from Exercise 1 on the lines below. Then circle each subject and underline each predicate.

1. _____

_____

2. _____

_____

3. _____

_____

4. _____

_____

5. _____

_____

KINDS OF SENTENCES

STATEMENTS

There are four kinds of sentences. The one you will write most often is a statement. A **statement** tells something or states a fact. It always ends with a period.

I am hungry.

Ottawa is the capital of Canada.

Jon earned five dollars at his lemonade stand.

Most students get to school by bus.

My mother works as a carpenter.

→ Your Turn 1

Write three statements of your own. Be sure that your sentences have a subject and a predicate. Remember to capitalize the first letter and put a period at the end.

1. _____

_____

2. _____

_____

3. _____

_____

QUESTIONS

If you want to ask something, you use a **question.** Questions always end with a question mark.

What time is it?

Where are you going?

Will you come to the game on Saturday?

Do you like strawberries?

How much does that comic book cost?

→ **Your Turn 2**

Now write three complete questions. Remember to capitalize the first letter and put a question mark at the end.

1. _____

_____

2. _____

_____

3. _____

_____

COMMANDS

If you want to tell someone to do something, you will use a **command.**
A command ends with a period. Since the subject of these sentences is
always "you," it is usually left out.

Take me to your leader.

Please get out your math books and turn to page 32.

Look both ways before you cross the street.

Drink the rest of your juice.

Try not to slam the door.

→ Your Turn 3

Try writing three commands. Don't forget to capitalize the first letter and put
a period at the end.

1. _____

_____

2. _____

_____

3. _____

_____

EXCLAMATIONS

Sometimes you will want to express a strong feeling about something. You will use an **exclamation.** Exclamations always end with an exclamation mark.

Your haircut looks fantastic!

I need to use the bathroom!

Don't drop your lunch tray!

The dragon is chasing him!

Wake up!

→ Your Turn 4

Now write three exclamations. Remember to capitalize the first letter and use an exclamation mark at the end.

1. _____

_____

2. _____

_____

3. _____

_____

Read these questions. Write a statement as an answer to each one. For some of these, you will need to make up or find the answer.

Example: Where is your homework?

My homework is in my school bag.

1. Why are you late?

2. When do you think Max will get here?

3. How many stars are on the American flag?

4. What happened to your finger?

This exercise gives you statements instead of questions. It is your job to write a question to go with each answer. Remember to begin each question with a capital and end with a question mark. Look at the example for help.

Example: How long will it take to get to Grandma's house?

It will take two hours to get there.

1. Tomorrow is a school day and you need to get to bed.

_____

_____

2. I found it in the grass by the road.

_____

_____

3. My friend gave it to me for my birthday.

_____

_____

4. Turn left and make the first right at the light.

_____

_____

Now you know the four kinds of sentences. Read each of these and decide whether it is a statement, question, command, or exclamation. Label the sentence **S**, **Q**, **C**, or **E**. Then add the correct punctuation mark at the end. There may be more than one right answer.

Examples : __Q__ What is your favorite pizza topping __?__

__C__ Don't forget to lock the door __.__

_____ 1. Watch out for that bee ___

_____ 2. How soon can we leave ___

_____ 3. I am excited ___

_____ 4. That flower is a tulip ___

_____ 5. Shut the windows before it starts raining ___

_____ 6. Thomas Edison invented the light bulb ___

_____ 7. Is Mars a planet or a star ___

_____ 8. Nobody really knows how lost dogs find their way home ___

_____ 9. The whale shark is the largest fish in the world ___

_____ 10. Watch out for that patch of ice ___

MAKING LISTS

Making lists is a great way to start writing. It helps you put your brain to work and organize your ideas. Look at the example lists below.

Playground games	Kinds of birds
kickball	robin
basketball	blue jay
hopscotch	woodpecker
jump rope	parrot
Simon says	sparrow

→ Exercise 1

Now it is your turn. Try to add ten things to each list. If you get stuck, you might want to work with a friend.

Things in the classroom

1. _____

2. _____

3. _____

4. _____

5. _____

6. _____

7. _____

8. _____

9. _____

10. _____

People who wear uniforms

1. _____
2. _____
3. _____
4. _____
5. _____

6. _____
7. _____
8. _____
9. _____
10. _____

Ways to exercise

1. _____
2. _____
3. _____
4. _____
5. _____

6. _____
7. _____
8. _____
9. _____
10. _____

Kinds of tools

1. _____

2. _____

3. _____

4. _____

5. _____

6. _____

7. _____

8. _____

9. _____

10. _____

Things that are green

1. _____

2. _____

3. _____

4. _____

5. _____

6. _____

7. _____

8. _____

9. _____

10. _____

Here are some more topics for making lists. On the next page, write down two of your favorites. Then add ten items to each list.

You can come back to this page when you need help finding a topic to write about. You can also use these topics to brainstorm for ideas.

Wild animals	Sticky things
Things you can draw with	Things you can recycle
Things made of metal	Things that glitter
Ways of crossing a stream	Animals that come out at night
How you help at home	Things you take turns doing
Things that make you laugh	Insects
Safety rules	Colors
Things made of wood	Kinds of weather
Musical instruments	Relatives
Animals that have horns	Your favorite movies
Things that melt	Kinds of trees
Things that are striped	Things that are soft
Things you do in the gym	Baby animals
Words that end in *y*	Kinds of costumes
Noisy places	Quiet places

Topic: _____

1. _____   6. _____

2. _____   7. _____

3. _____   8. _____

4. _____   9. _____

5. _____   10. _____

Topic: _____

1. _____   6. _____

2. _____   7. _____

3. _____   8. _____

4. _____   9. _____

5. _____   10. _____

SUPPORTING SENTENCES

Once you have organized your ideas, you can begin to write a paragraph. A paragraph is a group of sentences about the same topic. All of the longer things that you read—such as books, stories, and magazine articles—are made up of paragraphs.

After you have written a list, you can turn your ideas into sentences. These sentences are called **supporting sentences**. They support your topic by telling more about it.

Look at this example. It shows how the items in a list can be turned into supporting sentences.

Topic: Things to do at the beach

> 1. make sandcastles
>
> 2. collect shells
>
> 3. swim in the water

Things to do at the beach

S.S. 1. You can make sandcastles.

S.S. 2. You can collect shells.

S.S. 3. You can swim in the water.

Read the following lists. Then turn the items into sentences that support each topic.

1. Topic: Things to do at the mall

    1. shop

    2. eat

    3. go to the movies

Things to do at the mall

S.S.1. _____

S.S.2. _____

S.S.3. _____

2. Topic: Kinds of transportation

    1. train

    2. bus

    3. bicycle

Kinds of transportation

S.S.1. _____

S.S.2. _____

S.S.3. _____

3. Topic: Clothes you wear when it's cold

    1. hat

    2. mittens

    3. scarf

Clothes you wear when it's cold

    S.S.1. _____

    S.S.2. _____

    S.S.3. _____

4. Topic: Things to do at a party

    1. watch a video

    2. play games

    3. eat cake

Things to do at a party

    S.S.1. _____

    S.S.2. _____

    S.S.3. _____

5. Topic: Things you can see with a telescope

    1. stars

    2. the moon

    3. planets

Things you can see with a telescope

S.S.1. _____

S.S.2. _____

S.S.3. _____

6. Topic: Ways to stay cool when it is hot out

    1. sit in the shade

    2. drink cold water

    3. go for a swim

Ways to stay cool when it is hot out

S.S.1. _____

S.S.2. _____

S.S.3. _____

TOPICS

By now, you have written many lists on many topics. What would you do if you knew the items in the list, but did not know what the list was about?

What would you write as the topic for these lists? How would you decide?

rainy	milk
foggy	water
sunny	lemonade
cloudy	juice

Would you write **kinds of weather** and **things to drink**? Did you have another idea?

→ **Exercise 1**

Sometimes you may have some information, but you need to come up with a topic on your own. Read each of these lists. Try to think of the best topic for each one. Write it on the line. You might need to use more than one word for your topic.

1. _____

red

green

blue

yellow

white

2. _____

summer

fall

winter

spring

3. _____

    cows

    pigs

    horses

    sheep

    goats

4. _____

    sad

    happy

    scared

    surprised

5. _____

    paint brush

    water colors

    crayons

    pencils

    paper

6. _____

    vanilla

    chocolate

    strawberry

    cookies and cream

7. _____

    sore throat

    headache

    sneezing

    coughing

    fever

8. _____

    rose

    daffodil

    carnation

    daisy

9. _____

    house

    cabin

    teepee

    apartment

10. _____

    trout

    salmon

    bass

    tuna

TOPIC SENTENCES

You have already learned how to organize your ideas by using lists. You also know how to turn the items in a list into supporting sentences. The next step in writing a good paragraph is learning to write a topic sentence. **A topic sentence** tells what you are going to write about.

Do you remember this paragraph from page 54? Read it again.

Topic: Things to do at the beach

S.S. _You can make sandcastles._

S.S. _You can collect shells._

S.S. _You can swim in the water._

Here are three topic sentences to fit this paragraph.

There are many things to do at the beach.

You can always have fun at the beach.

Everybody enjoys the beach.

Read at these topic sentences again. Which one do you think is the best?

_____

_____

Turn these topics into topic sentences. It may be helpful for you to turn back to pages 55–56 to read the supporting sentences that you wrote for these lists.

When you are stuck, you can try this trick. Begin your topic sentence with **there is** or **there are.**

1. Topics: Things to do at the mall

   _____

   _____

2. Topic: Kinds of transportation

   _____

   _____

3. Topic: Clothes you wear when it's cold

   _____

   _____

4. Topic: Things to do at a party

   _____

   _____

These exercises give you the supporting sentences of a paragraph. Read each group of sentences. Try to write a good topic sentence for each. Look at the example for help.

Example: T.S. *Camels are interesting animals.*

        S.S. Camels can carry over 1,000 pounds.

        S.S. Camels can have one hump or two humps.

        S.S. A Camel can drink 27 gallons of water in only ten minutes.

1. T.S. _____

        S.S. You can have a snowball fight.

        S.S. You can make a snowman.

        S.S. You can go sledding.

_____

2. T.S. _____

        S.S. Sam always works quietly.

        S.S. Sam is polite to the teacher.

        S.S. Sam always does his homework.

_____

3. T.S. _____

        S.S. Last year Mr. Sing went to China.

        S.S. Mr. Sing spent the winter in Mexico.

        S.S. Mr. Sing plans to spend next summer in France.

_____

4. T.S. _____

    S.S. You need a raincoat.

    S.S. Put on your boots.

    S.S. Take an umbrella.

_____

5. T.S. _____

    S.S. You can write a letter.

    S.S. You can telephone.

    S.S. You can send a fax.

    S.S. You can send an e-mail.

_____

6. T.S. _____

    S.S. It can be fried sunny side up or over-easy.

    S.S. It can be boiled.

    S.S. It can be scrambled.

    S.S. It can be made into an omelet.

_____

7. T.S. _____

    S.S. Kim plays basketball after school.

    S.S. She belongs to the softball team.

    S.S. She goes bowling on the weekends.

    S.S. Kim is learning to play tennis.

_____

8. T.S. _____

    S.S. The leaves are turning red and yellow.

    S.S. The weather is getting colder.

    S.S. The days are getting shorter.

    S.S. Birds are beginning to fly south.

_____

9. T.S. _____

    S.S. My dad packed me a peanut butter and jelly sandwich.

    S.S. I also had a bag of carrot sticks.

    S.S. I had chocolate milk to drink.

    S.S. I had applesauce for dessert.

_____

10. T.S. _____

    S.S. You can take a taxi.

    S.S. You can get on the bus.

    S.S. The subway is very quick.

    S.S. Some people like to walk.

_____

CONCLUDING SENTENCES

A paragraph needs a topic sentence and supporting sentences. It also needs a concluding sentence at the end.

A concluding sentence gives one final idea about your topic. It can tell how you feel or what you think about your topic. It should not simply repeat your topic sentence.

Here is a topic sentence and four supporting sentences.

> T.S. There are many things you can do at the library.
>
> S.S. You can read new magazines.
>
> S.S. You can borrow books and movies.
>
> S.S. You can join a reading club.
>
> S.S. You can browse the Web.

Here are **two concluding sentences** to fit this paragraph.

> These are the things you can do at the library.
>
> I always look forward to going to the library.

Which of these do you think is a better concluding sentence? Why?

_____

_____

_____

→ **Exercise 1**

Go back to pages 62–64, where you wrote topic sentences. Read your topic sentences, the supporting sentences that follow, and add your own concluding sentence. Remember, your sentence should add a new idea to the paragraph, not just restate the topic sentence.

→ **Exercise 2**

Read the topic sentences and supporting sentences below. Then write a concluding sentence for each one.

1. T.S. I like to visit my grandfather.

   S.S. He takes me to the movies.

   S.S. He tells funny jokes.

   S.S. He likes to play games.

   C.S. _____

2. T.S. I did not sleep well last night.

   S.S. The dogs next door were barking.

   S.S. My alarm clock went off in the middle of the night.

   S.S. The rain made a lot of noise on the roof.

   C.S. _____

3. T.S. There are plenty of things to do in winter.

   S.S. I'll go sledding on the hill.

   S.S. I'll build a snowman.

   S.S. I'll play in the snow with my friends.

   C.S. _____

4. T.S. I wish I had a tree house.

   S.S. The view from high up would be great.

   S.S. It would be quiet and peaceful.

   S.S. Nobody would bother me up there.

   C.S. _____

5. T.S. We need to go to the grocery store.

   S.S. We are out of milk.

   S.S. I finished the orange juice this morning.

   S.S. There is no bread left.

   C.S. _____

6. T.S. Many things light our planet.

   S.S. The sun shines in the daytime.

   S.S. The moon shines at night.

   S.S. Thousands of stars brighten the night sky.

   C.S. _____

7. T.S. You can learn a lot about a place by looking at a map.

   S.S. Maps show the seas, rivers, and lakes.

   S.S. States and cities are marked.

   S.S. Maps show roads and railways.

   S.S. Some maps even show mountains.

   C.S. _____

8. T.S. Vegetables come from different parts of the plant.

   S.S. Carrots and turnips are roots.

   S.S. Lettuce and cabbage are leaves.

   S.S. Tomatoes and peppers are fruits.

   S.S. Cauliflower and broccoli are flowers.

   C.S. _____

9. T.S. Camping can be hard work.

   S.S. You have to put up the tent.

   S.S. You have to find wood and build a fire.

   S.S. Sometimes you have to get water from a spring.

   C.S. _____

10. T.S. If you have good balance, there are many sports you might enjoy.

    S.S. You might like in-line skating.

    S.S. You can ice skate in the winter.

    S.S. You can try gymnastics.

    C.S. _____

BASIC PARAGRAPHS

Now you understand how to write a topic sentence, supporting sentences, and a concluding sentence. These are the main parts of a basic paragraph.

A basic paragraph gives a complete picture of your own topic or idea. If you follow these steps, you will be able to compose your own.

1. Start with a list. Use the topic as a title.

2. Create a good topic sentence.

3. Check the three or four ideas on your list that you want to use to support your topic.

4. Turn each of them into a supporting sentence.

5. Add a concluding sentence.

Here is an example.

Topic: Things that need batteries

✓ watch

radio

✓ cameras

✓ flashlights

smoke alarms

T.S. There are many important things that will not work without batteries.

S.S. Wrist watches need batteries.

S.S. Flashlights need fresh batteries.

S.S. Cameras need batteries, too.

C.S. It is good to have extra batteries in case of an emergency.

Write a list on the following topic. Then follow the directions on page 69 to write your own paragraph below.

Topic: Good places for a class trip

_____

_____

_____

_____

T.S. _____

_____

S.S. _____

S.S. _____

S.S. _____

C.S. _____

_____

Write a list on a topic of your choice. Then follow the steps on page 69 to write your own paragraph below.

Topic: _____

_____

_____

_____

_____

_____

T.S. _____

_____

S.S. _____

S.S. _____

S.S. _____

C.S. _____

_____

FORMATTING PARAGRAPHS

When you write a paragraph, you need to add a title. Write the title in the middle of the line. Capitalize the first word and every important word. Do not underline it. Skip a line to start your paragraph.

Leave a space in front of the first sentence. This is called indenting. Look at the following paragraph. This is how it should look when it is written.

> ## Uses for Batteries
>
>   There are many important things that will not work without batteries. Wrist watches need batteries. Flashlights need fresh batteries. Camera batteries need to be changed even though they last a long time. It is good to have extra batteries in case of an emergency.

Practice writing titles. Use these list topics to create good titles for a paragraph. Remember to capitalize the first and all the important words.

1. Playground games

_____

2. Kinds of birds

_____

3. People who wear uniforms

_____

Go back to Exercise 1 on pages 71–72. Take your two paragraphs and rewrite them in the correct format below.

1. _____

_____

_____

_____

_____

2. _____

_____

_____

_____

_____

➔ Your Turn

Now write a paragraph on a topic of your choice. Be sure you have a title, topic sentence, supporting sentences, and a concluding sentence. Remember to indent the first line.

_____

_____

_____

_____

_____

ADJECTIVES

An adjective is a word that describes a noun. It can tell how someone or something looks, sounds, tastes, or feels to the touch. An adjective can also describe what you think about someone or something.

Read the following adjectives and the nouns they describe.

<u>shiny</u> penny   <u>wonderful</u> city

<u>squeaky</u> mouse   <u>sour</u> pickle

<u>delicious</u> pear   <u>beautiful</u> painting

<u>soft</u> bed   <u>favorite</u> outfit

<u>cold</u> morning   <u>loud</u> music

→ **Exercise 1**

Read each adjective again and decide whether it tells how something looks, sounds, tastes, feels, or what you think about it. Write it in the correct place in the chart below.

Looks	Sounds	Tastes	Feels	Think About

Choose two of the adjectives from page 76. Write a sentence for each one. Try to use a different noun from the one that is given.

1. _____

2. _____

1. Add an adjective to each of these nouns to tell how it **looks.**

_____ grass   _____ sunset

_____ drawing   _____ apple

_____ star   _____ bird

2. Add an adjective to each of these nouns to tell how it **tastes.**

_____ strawberry   _____ jelly

_____ soup   _____ chili

_____ lemon   _____ pickle

3. Add an adjective to each of these nouns to tell how it **sounds.**

_____ voice   _____ siren

_____ stream   _____ truck

_____ song   _____ rain

4. Add an adjective to each of these nouns to tell how it feels to the **touch.**

_____ water   _____ ice cube

_____ rock   _____ seaweed

_____ cactus   _____ marshmallow

5. Add an adjective to each of these nouns that tells what you **think about it.**

_____ neighborhood   _____ puppy

_____ friend   _____ storm

_____ movie   _____ birthday

In these sentences, fill in each blank with a good adjective.

1. The _____ man wore his _____ sweater.

2. Some _____ rabbits were snuggled in the grass.

3. She poured the _____ lemonade into the glasses.

4. The _____ horse lept over the _____ wall.

5. Today I sat in the _____ chair and read a book.

6. The _____ wind blew the _____ tree down.

7. They rode their _____ bicycles along the _____ sidewalk.

8. We watched the _____ baby crawling on the _____ carpet.

9. Many _____ flowers grow in the _____ park.

10. Last night there were many _____ stars in the _____ sky.

Sometimes you might want to add more than one adjective to a noun. Try adding two adjectives to each of these nouns. Then write a sentence using your words.

Example: _clear_ _blue_ water

We Saw fish swimming in the clear blue water.

1. _____ _____ hamster

   _____

2. _____ _____ pencil

   _____

3. _____ _____ bed

   _____

4. _____ _____ movie

   _____

5. _____ _____ story

   _____

ADVERBS

An adverb is a word that describes a verb. It can tell **how** or **when** or **where**. Adverbs usually come after the verb. Many of them end in **ly**.

These adverbs tell **how.**

walk **slowly**

leave **suddenly**

write **beautifully**

sing **happily**

drive **fast**

→ **Exercise 1**

Add an adverb of your own to tell **how.**

1. walk _____

2. leave _____

3. write _____

4. sing _____

5. drive _____

These adverbs tell **when.**

came **yesterday**

go **now**

arrive **soon**

travel **often**

play **today**

→ **Exercise 2**

Add an adverb of your own to tell **when**

1. came _____

2. go _____

3. arrive _____

4. travel _____

5. play _____

These adverbs tell **where**

swim **away**

come **here**

send **off**

climb **up**

walk **around**

→ **Exercise 3**

Add an adverb of your own to tell **where.**

1. swim _____

2. carry _____

3. come _____

4. send _____

5. put _____

Now choose five of the adverbs you wrote in Exercises 1, 2, and 3 and use them in sentences. You can use a different verb if you like.

1. _____

_____

2. _____

_____

3. _____

_____

4. _____

_____

5. _____

_____

Add adverbs to these sentences. Use this list to help you.

How	When	Where
fast	today	here
slowly	tomorrow	there
swiftly	yesterday	everywhere
softly	soon	nowhere
loudly	before	anywhere
happily	shortly	near

1. The ship will sail _____.

2. They rode _____ through the town.

3. She spoke _____.

4. The dog barked _____.

5. They sat _____ in the front row.

6. We unpacked all the boxes _____.

7. We waited _____ for the movie to begin.

8. The plane took off _____.

9. She arranged the flowers _____.

10. Please take the trash _____.

Sometimes an adverb starts a sentence. Try writing a sentence that begins with each of these adverbs.

Example: Now *I am ready to go.* _____

1. Unfortunately _____

_____

2. Tomorrow _____

_____

3. Suddenly _____

_____

4. Luckily _____

_____

5. Soon _____

_____

ADDING DETAILS

You can make your paragraphs more interesting by adding details. In this paragraph, the writer added details after the supporting sentences to give more information. The details are underlined.

My Family's Pets

My family has several pets. We have a dog named Frisky. <u>He has shiny black fur. He likes to play catch and can catch a Frisbee in the air.</u> Last summer we got a kitten from the animal shelter. <u>She is also black but has white paws. She likes to sleep on my bed.</u> We also have a fish tank in our living room. <u>The fish are small and brightly colored. When I feed them, they come rushing up to the surface.</u> Having pets in the house makes me happy.

→ Exercise 1

In the space below, copy the parts of the basic paragraph that are left when you take the details out.

T.S. _____

S.S. _____

S.S. _____

S.S. _____

C.S. _____

Read the following paragraph and underline the detail sentences. Then, in the space below, copy the parts of the paragraph that are left when you take the details out.

My Favorite Places

There are several places that I enjoy visiting. In the summer we go to the lake. The water is great for swimming. My mother and I like to fish. I also like to go the zoo, which is not far from my house. Our zoo has a place where you can watch the polar bears swimming under water. There is a big cage with many kinds of colorful birds. I like to go to the museum in the city. There is a giant bubble maker. There are also new computers that are fun to play with. All these places are special to me, and I learn something new every time I go there.

T.S. _____

S.S. _____

S.S. _____

S.S. _____

C.S. _____

These paragraphs have spaces for you to add details. Try to add two or three sentences after each support idea.

1.   **How I Help**

There are several things I do to help at home.

First, I try to keep my room neat. _____

_____

_____

Then I help at dinner. _____

_____

_____

Sometimes I help in the yard. _____

_____

_____

I try to help my family whenever I can.

2.   **The Playground**

   There is a great playground in our school yard.

It has a huge sandbox. _____

_____

_____

_____

There is a new swing set. _____

_____

_____

_____

There are places to climb. _____

_____

_____

_____

We like to play there every day.

3. **Dogs**

Dogs need a lot of care.

You have to feed them. _____

_____

_____

They must always have water. _____

_____

_____

If they have long hair, they need to be groomed. _____

_____

_____

They need exercise. _____

_____

_____

A dog can be a big responsibility.

Getting to School

People get to school in different ways.

Some children walk. _____

_____

_____

_____

Others come in cars driven by their parents. _____

_____

_____

_____

Most of us ride the school bus. _____

_____

_____

_____

How do you get to your school?

5.   **The Seasons**

     There is something special about every time of year.

In the winter, we enjoy the snow and ice. _____

_____

_____

In the spring, everybody likes watching the trees and flowers come to life.

_____

_____

In the summer, people can spend more time outdoors. _____

_____

_____

In the fall, the leaves turn beautiful colors. _____

_____

_____

My favorite time of year is _____ .

6.   Homework

Even though it is not always fun, homework is important.

It gives you a chance to practice what you have learned in school. _____

_____

_____

_____

It teaches you to be organized. _____

_____

_____

_____

Doing your homework helps you learn to work independently. _____

_____

_____

_____

You should do your best to complete all your homework every day.

Now write three paragraphs of your own. Add interesting details to each of your supporting ideas. You could write about three pets you have (or would like to have) or three places you enjoy visiting. You might like to use one of these subjects instead.

Favorite toys	Favorite books
Favorite places to eat	Things that make me happy
Things to do on a rainy day	Snacks
Kinds of parties	School rules
School trips	Things to put in a sandwich
Kinds of costumes	Musical instruments

1. _____

_____

_____

_____

_____

_____

2. _____

_____

_____

_____

_____

_____

3. _____

_____

_____

_____

_____

COMPOUND SENTENCES

A **compound sentence** is made up of two smaller sentences. These sentences are joined by a connecting word. The connecting word is usually **and**, **but**, or **or**.

Look at how these sentences join to make a compound sentence.

Sam plays the trumpet. Robert sings in the chorus.
Sam plays the trumpet, **and** Robert sings in the chorus.

I went to the party. I didn't stay long.
I went to the party, **but** I didn't stay long.

Nelly will be an astronaut. She will be a famous artist.
Nelly will be an astronaut, **or** she will be a famous artist.

→ Exercise 1

Fill in the blanks to complete these compound sentences.

1. The city _____ ,

   but the country _____ .

2. Turtles _____ ,

   but tortoises _____ .

3. Trains _____ ,

   but airplanes _____ .

97

Take these compound sentences apart. Write them as two separate sentences.

Example: We ate out last night, but tonight Dad is fixing dinner at home.

We ate out last night.

Tonight Dad is fixing dinner at home.

1. I will wash the dishes, and you can dry them.

_____

_____

2. I ran to catch the bus, but it left without me.

_____

_____

3. Ice cream is my favorite food, and I enjoy all the flavors.

_____

_____

4. My friend and I will play soccer this year, or we will join the drama club.

_____

_____

5. My cat sometimes stays out all night, but he is always home by morning.

_____

_____

6. The weather is getting warmer, and spring is on the way.

_____

_____

7. Tom can speak English with his mother, or he can speak Spanish with his grandmother.

_____

_____

8. Our family has moved a lot, and I have been to four different schools.

_____

_____

Now turn each pair of sentences into a compound sentence. Use a connecting word (**and**, **but**, or **or**). You will need to use a comma before the connecting word.

1. Today is sunny. It is supposed to rain tomorrow.

2. I would like to see the movie. It is no longer playing in our town.

3. The zoo is an interesting place. I look forward to going there.

4. I used to be afraid of thunderstorms. Now I enjoy watching the lightning.

5. Lee may go to the movies. She may go bowling.

6. At first I did not understand the math problem. The teacher explained it.

7. Dad went to the store. It was closed.

Now write some compound sentences of your own. Use **and**, **but**, or **or** to join the parts together. Use a comma before the connecting word. Remember to start your sentences with a capital letter and end with a punctuation mark.

1. _____

_____

2. _____

_____

3. _____

_____

4. _____

_____

5. _____

_____

TELLING *WHY*

You can expand your sentences by telling **why.** A good way to tell the reason for something is to use the word **because**.

Martin is studying **because** he has a science quiz tomorrow.

I will lend you my bike **because** you are my friend.

The doctor told me to stay home **because** I need to rest.

Exercise 1

Finish these by telling **why**.

1. I feel happy because _____.

2. We were late because _____.

3. We cannot have a picnic today because _____.

4. We could not open the door because _____.

5. They won the game because _____.

Now write five sentences of your own that tell **why**.

1. _____

_____

2. _____

_____

3. _____

_____

4. _____

_____

5. _____

_____

TELLING *WHEN*

Sometimes it is important to tell **when** something happens. There are many ways of telling when.

You can use a time word, such as **when**, **before**, **after**, or **until**.

> The teacher calls on her **when** she raises her hand.
>
> Wipe your boots **before** you come in the house.
>
> I will call you **after** I finish my homework.
>
> Jon used training wheels **until** he learned to ride a bike.

→ Exercise 1

Fill in the blanks to complete these sentences that tell **when**.

1. The dog always barks until _____.

2. They were happy after _____.

3. We can go skating when _____.

4. Clean your room before _____.

5. The mail carrier came before _____.

Write five sentences that tell **when**. Remember to use a capital letter at the beginning and a punctuation mark at the end.

1. _____

_____

2. _____

_____

3. _____

_____

4. _____

_____

5. _____

_____

You can use the part that tells **when** at the beginning of your sentences as well. When you turn the sentences around this way, you need to use a comma after the words that tell when.

> **When** she raises her hand, the teacher calls on her
>
> **Before** you come in the house, wipe your boots.
>
> **After** I finish my homework, I will call you.
>
> **Until** he learned to ride a bike, Jon used training wheels.

→ Exercise 2

Fill in these blanks to complete sentences that tell **when.** In these sentences, the words that tell when come first.

1. After it rains, _____.

2. Until breakfast is ready, _____.

3. When the moon is full, _____.

4. Before you leave, _____.

5. Before we had a computer, _____.

Look at your sentences from page 105. Write your sentences again. This time, use the part that tells when at the beginning. Remember to use a comma after the words that tell when, a capital letter at the beginning, and a punctuation mark at the end.

1. _____

_____

2. _____

_____

3. _____

_____

4. _____

_____

5. _____

_____

There are many other words that you can use to tell **when.** Write two sentences for each of these other time words.

1. whenever

_____

_____

2. as soon as

_____

_____

3. ever since

_____

_____

4. while

_____

_____

5. since

_____

_____

GIVING CONDITIONS

Sometimes you will need to give a different type of information, or state a condition. **Condition sentences** use the word **if**.

You can pick those apples **if** they are ripe.

The team will win the game **if** they practice.

Spot will come **if** you call him.

→ **Exercise 1**

Complete these **if** sentences by stating a condition.

1. That glass will break if _____ .

2. I will be happy if _____ .

3. She will be here soon if _____ .

4. Robert will go to the party if _____ .

Unless is another word that states a condition.

The seed will not grow **unless** it has water and light.

We'll go on a hike **unless** it is raining.

You cannot buy that hat **unless** you have saved enough money.

→ **Exercise 2**

Complete these **unless** sentences.

1. I cannot see the blackboard unless _____

_____ .

2. They will go camping unless _____

_____ .

3. He will deliver their paper unless _____

_____ .

4. She cannot buy a bicycle unless _____

_____ .

5. We will visit you unless _____

_____ .

Just like sentences that tell you **why** or **when**, the parts of condition sentence can also be switched. Finish these **if** and **unless** sentences.

1. If the cat has fleas, _____.

2. If they enjoy camping out, _____.

3. If that dog is housebroken, _____.

4. If your backpack is very heavy, _____.

5. If you wake up early, _____.

6. Unless I made a mistake, _____.

7. Unless you have x-ray vision, _____.

8. Unless those tomatoes are ripe, _____.

9. Unless you are really sick, _____.

10. Unless that frog jumps into the water, _____.

Now write five condition sentences of your own using **if** or **unless.** If you use the condition word in the beginning of your sentence, remember to use a comma.

1. _____

   _____

2. _____

   _____

3. _____

   _____

4. _____

   _____

5. _____

   _____

EXAMPLE PARAGRAPHS

There are five kinds of paragraphs that are important for you to learn.

The first one is called **an example paragraph**. It gives examples of things.

Read this example paragraph.

Recycling

Many things can be recycled. At home, we save aluminum cans. Many plastic containers can also be recycled. In school, we put used papers in a separate bin. I try to recycle whenever I can.

Add items to each list to start an example paragraph.

Ways to make friends

1. _____

2. _____

3. _____

4. _____

5. _____

Delicious things to eat

1. _____

2. _____

3. _____

4. _____

5. _____

Important safety rules

1. _____

2. _____

3. _____

4. _____

5. _____

Places that charge admission

1. _____

2. _____

3. _____

4. _____

5. _____

Take your favorite list and turn in into a basic example paragraph. You will need a topic sentence, three supporting sentences, and a concluding sentence. Choose the supporting sentences from the ideas on your list. Remember to give your paragraph a title and to indent the first sentence.

_____

_____

_____

_____

_____

_____

_____

_____

Your Turn 2

Write a basic example paragraph of your own. Choose a topic that interests you and give three examples.

_____

_____

_____

_____

_____

_____

_____

_____

_____

PROCESS PARAGRAPHS

A process paragraph gives directions or tells someone how to do something. Recipes, video game instructions, and directions to your friend's house are all process paragraphs.

Read this example process paragraph. Try to follow the instructions in the space below.

Drawing a House

First, get a pencil. In the middle of the box, draw a square. Next, draw a large triangle on top of the square and a tall rectangle inside the bottom of the square. Last, draw two smaller squares on either side of the rectangle.

Was this process paragraph clear? How well were you able to follow these directions?

Add items to each list to start a process paragraph. Remember to put the steps in the correct order. It is often helpful to use the words **first**, **next**, **then**, and **last**.

How to plant seeds

1. _____

2. _____

3. _____

4. _____

5. _____

How to sharpen a pencil

1. _____

2. _____

3. _____

4. _____

5. _____

How to set the table

1. _____

2. _____

3. _____

4. _____

5. _____

How to play tag

1. _____

2. _____

3. _____

4. _____

5. _____

Take your favorite list and turn in into a basic process paragraph. You will need a topic sentence, supporting sentences, and a concluding sentence. Remember to give your paragraph a title and to indent the first sentence.

_____

_____

_____

_____

_____

_____

_____

_____

Think of something you know how to do well and write your own process paragraph. Try to use three, four, or even five supporting sentences.

_____

_____

_____

_____

_____

_____

_____

REASON PARAGRAPHS

The next kind of paragraph that you should know is **a reason paragraph**. This kind of paragraph gives reasons for things and often uses the word **because**. Read this example reason paragraph.

The Summer

Almost everyone enjoys the summer because there are so many things to do. You can spend the day at the beach. You can picnic in the park with your friends. School is out, so you can go on vacation or visit your relatives. I can't wait for the summer to arrive.

Can you think of other reasons to enjoy the summer? Write them on the lines below.

_____

_____

_____

Complete each list to start a basic reason paragraph.

Why students should do their homework

1. _____

2. _____

3. _____

4. _____

5. _____

Reasons for saving money

1. _____

2. _____

3. _____

4. _____

5. _____

Reasons for visiting the city

1. _____

2. _____

3. _____

4. _____

5. _____

Reasons for going to the library

1. _____

2. _____

3. _____

4. _____

5. _____

Take your favorite list and turn it into a basic reason paragraph. Write a topic sentence, then turn your three reasons into supporting sentences. Add a concluding sentence at the end. Remember to include a title and to indent the first sentence.

_____

_____

_____

_____

_____

_____

_____

_____

→ Your Turn 2

Read your paragraph again and think of ways that you can expand it. You can expand your sentences by adding adjectives, adverbs, telling why or when, or giving a condition. You can also expand your paragraph by adding details to each of your supporting ideas.

_____

_____

_____

_____

_____

_____

_____

_____

PERSUASION PARAGRAPHS

A persuasion paragraph is a special kind of reason paragraph. You write this kind of paragraph when you want to convince somebody to do something.

Read this example persuasion paragraph.

Bedtime

I need to have a later bedtime. All my friends stay up until nine o'clock. If I did not have to go to bed so early, I would have more time to do my homework and to read. Also, Dad sometimes gets home late from work and I would like to spend more time with him at night. Please change my bedtime.

What are the three reasons this writer gives for wanting a later bedtime?

1. _____

2. _____

3. _____

Read this persuasion paragraph and answer the questions that follow.

Sleepovers

Next week is my birthday, and I would like to have four friends come for a sleepover. They would all bring sleeping bags so you would not have to make up any beds. We will help fix supper and clean up afterwards. After supper we will go to the den and quietly watch a video. We will promise to go to sleep by 10:30. I hope you will let me have a sleepover party.

1. How many reasons does this writer give?

_____

_____

_____

2. Which do you think is the best one? Why?

_____

_____

_____

Read this persuasion paragraph and answer the questions that follow.

A Tree House

I would like to build a tree house in the yard. It would make our yard a special place for me and my friends. We are old enough to be careful when we climb up there. When I want to be alone, I would have a great, safe place to go. It would not cost much since we have some lumber in the basement. Mom is good at building things, and I would help her. A tree house in the yard would make me very happy.

1. What do you think is the best reason for a tree house?

_____

_____

_____

2. Can you think of any others?

_____

_____

_____

Read this persuasion paragraph and answer the questions that follow.

A Kitten

I know we can't have a dog because nobody is home during the day. But couldn't I have a kitten? Kittens can be alone all day. I would feed it and empty the litter box every day. It could sleep in my room and keep me company at night. Kittens don't cost anything if you adopt one from the animal shelter. Please let me have a kitten.

1. What do you think is the best reason for a kitten?

_____

_____

_____

2. Can you think of any others?

_____

_____

_____

Write a persuasion paragraph of your own on one of the following topics. If you wish, you may make your own topic.

You would like to take piano lessons.

You want to go to the circus with a friend even though it is a school night.

You would like to borrow ten dollars from your brother or sister.

You would like your school to move your bus stop nearer to your house.

You want to invite everyone in your class to a pool party this summer.

_____

_____

_____

_____

_____

_____

_____

COMPARING AND CONTRASTING

Comparing and contrasting is a special kind of writing. It asks you to write about how two things are alike and how they are different.

Read this example. The first and last paragraphs are the beginning and the ending. The second paragraph tells how these two things are alike. The third paragraph tells how they are different.

Our Houses

My friend Max and I live on a busy street near our school. The street is very pretty and has many trees.

Our homes are alike in many ways. Both our houses are made of brick and both are painted white. They both have two stories, with the living room and kitchen downstairs and the bedrooms upstairs. Both houses have basements and both have a small front porch.

The houses are different in many ways. My house has blue shutters and a green door. Max's house has black shutters and a red door. My porch is screened, but Max's is not. Max's basement has been fixed up to use as a play room. Mine has nothing in it but a washing machine and a dryer.

Max and I both like our own houses. We also like to live next door to one another so that we can visit each other whenever we'd like.

Read the following paragraphs. Then complete the exercises that follow.

Friends

I have two special friends at school. We have been friends since kindergarten. Their names are Kim and Josie.

Both my friends are eight years old. They are about the same height and they both have brown hair. They both live in my town. They are both fun to visit and they are always happy to see me.

Josie's parents are Puerto Rican, and they speak Spanish at home. Her parents came from Puerto Rico before she was born. Kim's parents have always lived in America, and she only speaks English. Josie always wears her hair in braids, but Kim always wears hers in a ponytail. Josie loves to read, but Kim loves to play video games.

I am lucky to have such good friends. I hope we will be friends forever.

1. Make a list that tells how Josie and Kim are the same.

_____

_____

_____

_____

_____

2. Now make a list that tells how Josie and Kim are different.

_____

_____

_____

_____

Now write a comparison/contrast paragraph of your own. Remember, the first paragraph is the beginning, the second paragraph tells how the two things are the same, the third paragraph tells how they are different, and the last paragraph is the ending.

Compare and contrast the following or choose two things on your own.

two playgrounds	two movies
two parks	two video games
two trucks	two living rooms
two books	two pairs of shoes
two seasons	two kinds of birds

_____

_____

_____

_____

_____

_____

SHORT ANSWER QUESTIONS

You can often use the kinds of writing you have learned when you answer questions in your homework assignments or on tests. To start, it helps to turn the question into a sentence. Then decide what kind of paragraph you will need to write. Finally, answer the question with several supporting sentences.

Look at these examples.

How do animals survive the winter?

Here you can give **examples.**

> Animals survive the winter in many ways. Bears hibernate. Squirrels store food. Many birds migrate south.

How can you cross a busy street safely?

Here you describe the **process.**

> It is important to cross a busy street safely. You should cross at the crosswalk. Wait until you see the walk signal, even you think there are no cars coming. Remember to look both ways before starting across.

Why did pioneers want to move west?

Here you will give **reasons.**

> The pioneers moved west because they needed more land to farm. Some people were not happy in the new cities in the east. Also, many were excited by the discovery of gold.

Decide how you would answer these questions if they were part of a homework assignment or on a test. Label the questions **example, process,** or **reason**. There may be more than one right answer.

1. _____ Why did dinosaurs become extinct?

2. _____ How did the Egyptians preserve their dead?

3. _____ What are the best inventions in the past 100 years?

4. _____ Why do people have to pay taxes?

5. _____ Why is pollution a problem?

Go back to each of the questions above. Turn each one into a topic sentence and write it on the lines below.

1. _____

2. _____

3. _____

4. _____

5. _____

Choose two of the questions from Exercise 1 that you know the most about. Rewrite the question as a topic sentence and give three supporting sentences for each.

1. _____

_____

_____

_____

_____

2. _____

_____

_____

_____

_____

By now you are learning new and interesting things in science and social studies. Ask your teacher to give you a question to answer. Then write a short answer paragraph for each question.

_____

_____

_____

_____

_____

_____

_____

_____

_____

NARRATION

Sometimes you will want to write about events and experiences—things that happened at home, in your town, or in your school. You might want to write about an experience you had—alone or with your family. This kind of writing is called **narration.**

When you do this kind of writing, you will want to answer the five Ws.

Who was involved?

What happened?

Where did it happen?

When did it happen?

Why was it important?

Here is an example narrative paragraph.

A Maple Syrup Factory

Last week we went to the maple syrup factory in Ottawa. The guide told us all about maple sugar. We saw maple trees and the plastic pipes they use now instead of buckets. We saw the sap being boiled in very large tanks. The guide gave us each a sample to taste. It takes forty gallons of sap to make one gallon of syrup. Making syrup does not harm the tree. I learned a lot of interesting things about maple syrup.

Read this paragraph. Did the writer remember to tell about the five Ws? Underline **who**, **what**, **where**, **when**, and **why**. Then write the information below.

Possums

Yesterday I was riding my bike along the trail when I saw an amazing sight. I watched a possum, on the side of the trail. It was a mother possum, and she had five tiny babies on her back clinging to her tail. I was close enough to count them before she disappeared into the tall grass. I hope that I will see the possum family again soon.

Who _____

What _____

Where _____

When _____

Why _____

Read this paragraph. Did the writer remember to tell about the five Ws? Underline **who**, **what**, **where**, **when**, and **why**. Then write the information below.

A Special Event

Last Sunday my dad took me to a classical music concert. It was the first time I have ever seen a whole orchestra with all the different instruments. The musicians were all dressed in black. The conductor stood up on a platform where the musicians could see him. He kept time and told the different musicians when to start and stop playing. I enjoyed watching them all, especially the percussionist. She clashed the cymbals at the very end of the song. Everybody applauded, and the conductor and orchestra bowed to us. I felt very lucky to go to such a special event.

Who _____

What _____

Where _____

When _____

Why _____

Think about something that happened to you in school that you would like to write about. You can write about your very first day, a special class trip that you took, or you can think of your own topic. First, write down the five Ws. Then write a complete paragraph with a topic sentence, supporting sentences, and a concluding sentence.

Who _____

What _____

Where _____

When _____

Why _____

_____

_____

_____

_____

_____

_____

_____

Think about something that happened to you at home that you would like to write about. First, write down the five Ws. Then write a complete paragraph with a topic sentence, supporting sentences, and a concluding sentence.

Who _____

What _____

Where _____

When _____

Why _____

_____

_____

_____

_____

_____

_____

FRIENDLY LETTERS

It is fun to write a letter to a friend or relative. People love getting letters. Some people save all the letters they receive.

You may want to write a letter to thank someone for something or to tell them some news. These are fun paragraphs to write.

Here are two sample paragraphs that thank someone.

> Thank you for the sweater. Blue is my favorite color. It fits perfectly. It is very special to me because you made it yourself. I will wear it on the first day of school.

> Thank you for taking me to the zoo yesterday. It was fun seeing the polar bears being fed. I liked watching the monkeys swing around in their cage. The baby giraffe was very cute. I always love visiting the zoo.

Write a paragraph to thank someone for something. Choose from the list of topics below.

Someone has given you a birthday gift.

Someone has done a special favor for you.

Someone has taken you to a museum.

Someone has taken you to a concert.

Someone special has come to visit you.

_____

_____

_____

_____

_____

_____

_____

_____

Here are two sample paragraphs that tell some news.

Today is rainy day. Mom says we need the rain for things to grow. This morning I helped my sister bake cookies. This evening we are going to rent a video. Rainy days can be a lot of fun.

You'll never guess what happened yesterday. I slipped on some ice and hurt my wrist. Dad took me to the hospital. The doctor took an x-ray. He said it is a just a sprain. The nurse bandaged my wrist and hand. Luckily, it was my left wrist, and I can still write this letter.

Now write a paragraph that tells someone some news. Choose from the list of topics below.

Tell what you plan to do on a warm, sunny day.

Your team has just won a game.

You studied hard and did well on a test at school.

You are sick and have to stay home.

You are getting a new pet.

_____

_____

_____

_____

_____

_____

_____

THE PARTS OF A LETTER

Now you already know how to write the paragraphs (called the body) of a letter. This section will teach you how to format your letter.

A letter has four parts.

1. **The heading**

   Begin by writing your address in the top left-hand side of your paper. You do this so that the person you are writing to will know where to send a reply. Skip a line after the address and write the date.

2. **The greeting**

   The greeting is the part of your letter that says hello. Capitalize every word in the greeting, too. Add a comma at the end.

3. **The body**

   Start your first paragraph right underneath the greeting. Remember to indent. If you have more than one paragraph in your letter, skip a line and indent.

4. **The closing**

   The closing says goodbye. Skip a line and capitalize the first letter. Skip another line and sign your name.

Here is an example friendly letter. The four parts have been labeled.

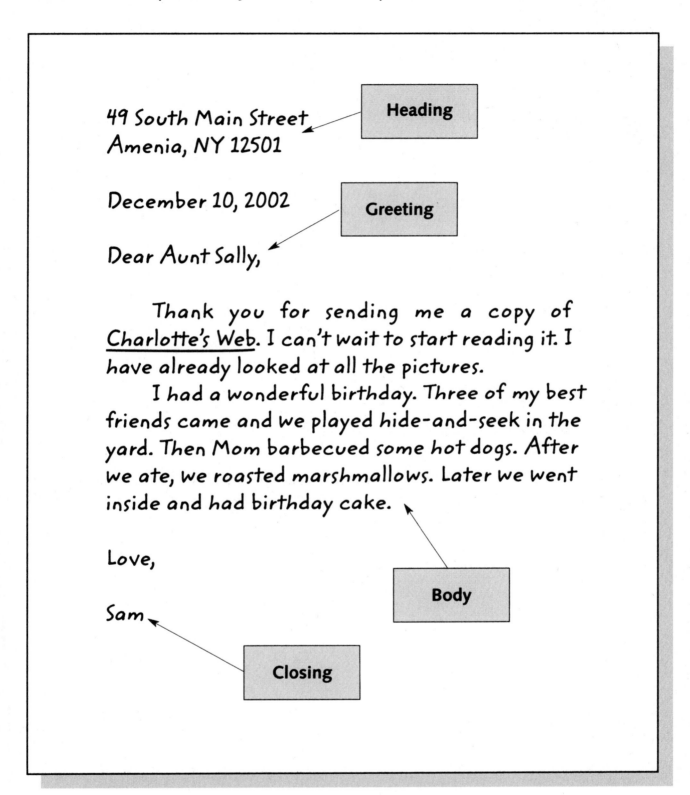

49 South Main Street
Amenia, NY 12501

December 10, 2002

Dear Aunt Sally,

    Thank you for sending me a copy of Charlotte's Web. I can't wait to start reading it. I have already looked at all the pictures.
    I had a wonderful birthday. Three of my best friends came and we played hide-and-seek in the yard. Then Mom barbecued some hot dogs. After we ate, we roasted marshmallows. Later we went inside and had birthday cake.

Love,

Sam

Heading

Greeting

Body

Closing

Read Sam's letter to Aunt Sally again. Underline each capital letter. Circle each comma. Then box each period.

Practice writing the parts of a letter.

1. Look at these headings.

420 Birdsong Street
San Antonio, TX 78258

July 6, 2003

126 North Road
Apt. 7B
Island City, NJ 31206

September 2, 2002

Practice writing the heading of a letter. Write your address and today's date on the lines below. Remember to skip a line for the date. Remember to use capital letters and commas in the right places.

_____

_____

_____

_____

_____

2. Look at these greetings.

Dear Tyler,

Dear Uncle Ed,

Dear Dad,

Practice writing three greetings. Write two to your friends and one to a relative.

_____

_____

_____

3. Look at these closings.

Love,
Pam

Your friend,
Seth

Practice writing two closings in the middle of the line. Don't forget to sign your name underneath.

_____

_____

_____

Write a letter to your friend inviting him or her to a party at your house. Be sure to use the correct heading, greeting, and closing, and be sure to give all the information your friend needs.

_____

_____

_____

_____

_____

_____

_____

_____

_____

Write a letter to a relative to tell about a trip that you took. Remember to use the correct heading, greeting, and closing.

_____

_____

_____

_____

_____

_____

_____

_____

_____

_____

FORMAL LETTERS

People also write letters to people that they do not know to give their opinion or to ask for information. People write letters to companies about their products. They write letters to politicians about their city or state. This kind of letter is called **a formal letter**.

When you write a formal letter, it is good to introduce yourself in the first sentence since the person you are writing to probably does not know you.

Here are two paragraphs that you may see in a formal letter. The first one asks for information. The second one gives an opinion.

> My name is Stacey Goldman. I am in fourth grade at Elm Street Elementary School. Our class is studying panda bears. Does the zoo have any information about panda bears that we can use in our class? We would like it if you would send us some.

> My name is Tom Lopez. My family watches your television program every week. We really enjoy learning about different places in the world. My favorite episode was when you explored the tomb of King Tut. I am a big fan of yours.

Write the paragraph of a formal letter. Here are some ideas.

Ask a police officer for bicycle safety information.

Ask your favorite actor for his or her autograph.

Ask someone for information about a place you'd like to visit.

Tell your librarian that the library should subscribe to more magazines.

Tell the mayor that your city should have a new park.

_____

_____

_____

_____

_____

_____

_____

_____

THE PARTS OF A FORMAL LETTER

The format of a formal letter is similar to the format of a friendly letter. There are only a few differences. Look at this example.

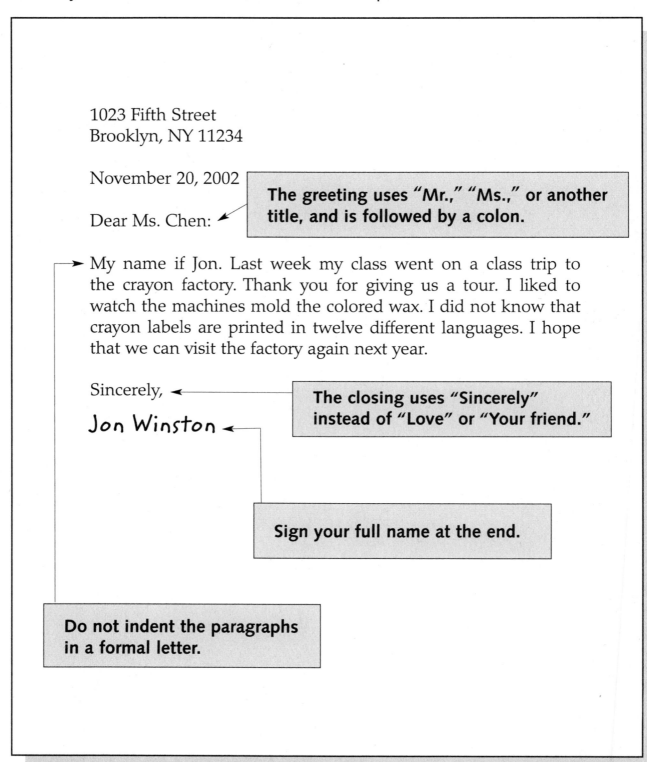

1023 Fifth Street
Brooklyn, NY 11234

November 20, 2002

Dear Ms. Chen:

The greeting uses "Mr.," "Ms.," or another title, and is followed by a colon.

My name if Jon. Last week my class went on a class trip to the crayon factory. Thank you for giving us a tour. I liked to watch the machines mold the colored wax. I did not know that crayon labels are printed in twelve different languages. I hope that we can visit the factory again next year.

Sincerely,

Jon Winston

The closing uses "Sincerely" instead of "Love" or "Your friend."

Sign your full name at the end.

Do not indent the paragraphs in a formal letter.

Read these formal greetings. Then practice writing formal greetings using the names of three of your teachers. Don't forget to use Mr., Ms., or Mrs. and a colon.

Dear Dr. Smith: _____

Dear Ms. Chang: _____

Dear Mr. Portman: _____

Read these formal closings. Then practice writing three formal closings in the middle of the line. Sign your whole name after each one.

Sincerely, _____
Michael Smith

_____

Yours sincerely, _____
Susan Johnson

_____

Yours truly, _____
Charles Wright

_____

Write a letter to your principal or your teacher to tell them that you think you should have a longer lunch period. Remember to use the correct heading, greeting, and closing.

_____

_____

_____

_____

_____

_____

_____

_____

_____

_____

This time, write a letter that you plan to send. It can be to a friend or relative, or it can be to someone that you do not know. You can brainstorm with your class for ideas. After you have written it, copy it to a separate piece of paper in your best handwriting.

Be sure to use the correct heading, greeting, and closing. You will also need to write the person's address on the envelope. Do this the same way that you wrote the heading, and add the person's name to the top.

_____

_____

_____

_____

_____

_____

_____

_____

_____

REVISING AND EDITING

After you have written a paragraph or a letter, you should always go back and check for mistakes.

Here are some things to check for.

1. Check for proper punctuation.
   - A statement ends with a period.
   - A question ends with a question mark.
   - A command ends with a period.
   - An exclamation ends with an exclamation mark.

2. Check for capital letters.
   - Capitalize the first letter of a sentence.
   - Capitalize the names of specific people, places, and things.
   - When you are writing a letter, capitalize the heading, greeting, closing, and the words in the address.

3. Check your spelling. Spelling mistakes are often hard to find. Your teacher may help you by putting a dot near a line that has a spelling mistake so that you can try to fix it on your own.

4. Check for sentence fragments and run-on sentences. You will read more about these on the following pages.

SENTENCE FRAGMENTS

Sentence fragments are sentences that are not complete. Remember, a complete sentence needs a subject and a predicate.

Look at these sentence fragments. Then look at the complete sentences that follow.

Fragment: Under the stars.
Sentence: We camped out under the stars.

Fragment: Before we knew it.
Sentence: Before we knew it, the basement was flooded.

→ Exercise 1

Fix these sentence fragments by making them complete sentences. Remember that a sentence must have a subject and a predicate.

1. When the wind blows.

   _____

2. After you finish supper.

   _____

3. In the morning.

   _____

4. As soon as they are ready.

   _____

5. Since it is dark.

_____

6. Before we leave.

_____

7. Until you can save some money.

_____

8. Because the floor is still wet.

_____

9. If my mom will let me.

_____

10. Whenever she comes to our house.

_____

RUN-ON SENTENCES

Another common mistakes that writers make is called a **run-on sentence**. A run-on sentence is more than one sentence that is grouped together. Run-ons need to be broken into two or even three separate sentences. You can sometimes turn them into compound sentences by adding **and** or **but**.

Look at these examples of run-on sentences and the complete sentences that follow.

Run-on: I like school my favorite subject is science.
Complete: I like school. My favorite subject is science.

Run-on: My head aches I have a runny nose.
Complete: My head aches, and I have a runny nose.

Run-on: Henry likes pancakes he prefers waffles.
Complete: Henry likes pancakes, but he prefer waffles.

➔ **Exercise 1**

Fix these run-on sentences. Break them up into separate sentences or use **and** or **but** to connect them.

1. We have a new dog it is a terrier.

_____

2. I cannot do this please help me.

_____

3. We have new neighbors they moved in yesterday.

_____

4. It is late we need to go home now.

_____

5. Dinner is ready wash your hands come to the kitchen.

_____

6. I did not like that movie it was too boring.

_____

7. She is always cheerful she has lots of friends.

_____

8. Walk carefully the sidewalk is icy.

_____

9. We read the book it was about polar bears.

_____

10. Some people believe in ghosts I do not.

_____

PRACTICE WRITING

Here are some prompts that you can use to help you practice writing. Once you have decided what you are going to write about, make a list to help you organize your ideas. Turn your topic into a topic sentence. Next, turn your list items into at least three supporting sentences. Then add a concluding sentence. Finally, give your paragraph a title. You might want to expand your paragraph by adding details.

Remember to check your paragraph for capitalization, punctuation, and spelling mistakes.

1. Imagine that you have a new neighbor from another country. Explain why your neighborhood is a good place to live.

2. Choose your favorite season and describe what you like to do during that time.

3. People sometimes show that they are very brave. Pick a time that you acted bravely and tell about it.

4. Write about a day when you felt that everything went wrong.

6. Choose a character in a book that you have read and explain why you like him or her.

7. Tell about a member of your family whom you admire.

8. Tell about a special memory that you have.

9. People learn new things in school. Tell about something new that you would like to learn about this year.

10. Imagine that you are going to give a birthday party for your best friend. Tell how you would do it.

11. Write about what you would like to be when you are older. Tell why.

12. Many people have a routine when they get ready for school in the morning. Write the steps that you take to get ready.

13. It is important to take care of the earth. Tell what you and your class do to help.

14. Write about the things that can go wrong at school.

15. Pretend that you have been granted three wishes. Tell what they are.

16. Write about a storm that you have experienced. Tell what happened before, during, and after.

17. Tell about a game or a sport that you enjoy. What is the object of the game? What are the rules?

18. Tell about the things you can do indoors when it is raining.

19. Write about something you own that is precious to you. Where did you get it? Why is it so special?

20. Suppose you could build your own house. Tell where you would build it, what it would look like, and what you would put inside.

21. What are three inventions you could not do without? Explain why.

22. Imagine that you are a planning a family vacation. Where would you go and what would you do there?

23. You have just learned that there will be no school tomorrow. How will you spend the day?

24. People are often scared of things like snakes or thunderstorms. Is there anything that scares you? Tell why.

25. It is fun to dress up. Tell about a costume that you have worn.

26. Why do you think some people like to live near the ocean, a lake, river, or stream.

27. Why is it important for people to plant trees?

28. Is there a time in history that you think would be fun to visit? What would you do there?

29. Is there a famous person you would like to meet? What would you say to him or her if you did?

30. Have you ever wished that you could become invisible? Name three things that you would do if you could.